W9-BYL-531

Queen Elizabeth II

Queen Elizabeth II

By Robert Green

A First Book

FranklinWatts

A DIVISION OF GROLIER PUBLISHING

New York   London   Hong Kong   Sydney

Danbury, Connecticut

Photographs ©: AP/Wide World Photos: 11, 22, 30; Corbis-Bettmann: 48, 54; Oistin Macbride/Corbis-Bettmann: cover, 44; Press Association/Topham Picture Source: cover, 3 (John Stillwell); Reuters/Corbis-Bettmann: 53; Superstock, Inc.: 35 (National Portrait Gallery, London, England) 8, 9, 17, 26, 27, 46; Topham Picture Source: 21, 25, 41, 51; UPI/Corbis-Bettmann: cover, 6, 10, 12, 14, 15, 18, 28, 33, 36, 38, 42, 57.

Library of Congress Cataloging-in-Publication Data

Green, Robert, 1969–
        Queen Elizabeth II / by Robert Green
                p. cm.—(A First book)
        Includes bibliographical references and index.
        Summary: Examines the life of the present British queen, discussing
her royal upbringing, the job she inherited, her commitment to the monarchy,
and her highly publicized family.
        ISBN 0-531-20303-4
        1. Elizabeth II, Queen of Great Britain, 1926–   —Juvenile literature.
2. Queens—Great Britain—Biography—Juvenile literature.   [1. Elizabeth II,
Queen of Great Britain, 1926–   2. Kings, queens, rulers, etc.]   I. Title.
II. Series.
DA590.G72   1997
941.085'092—dc21   96-41099
                                                                              CIP
                                                                              AC

Contents

I
Windsors at War 7

II
Elizabeth Regina 19

III
The Queen and the Commonwealth 31

IV
The Silver Jubilee 37

V
An Uncertain Future 49

For More Information 59

Royal Family Tree 60

Index 62

Elizabeth in her
ATS uniform in 1945

I

WINDSORS AT WAR

The women who volunteered for the Auxiliary Territorial Service (ATS) during World War II wore plain khaki uniforms and, from a distance, looked more or less alike. But Number 230873, Second Subaltern Elizabeth Alexandra Mary Windsor, was very different indeed. Her father was King George VI, and she was heir to the throne of Britain. She became Queen Elizabeth II of Great Britain in 1952 and continues to reign today.

When war broke out in 1939, the governing body of Britain, called Parliament, suggested that Princess Elizabeth and her younger sister Margaret Rose set sail for Canada, where they would be far from danger. Elizabeth's mother replied, "The children won't leave without me; I won't leave without the king; and the king will never leave."

The stark days of war greatly shaped Elizabeth's character. She learned, above all, the importance of duty and the necessity for the royal family to lead Britain by example. Elizabeth

was determined to devote herself to the service of Britain and to the traditions of the British royal family, known as the House of Windsor.

The British royalty was primarily of German descent. The family name of Elizabeth's grandfather, George V, was Saxe-Coburg-Gotha. At the outbreak of World War I in 1914, when war was declared against Germany, he decided to change it to something a little

Windsor Castle, Berkshire, was originally a Norman
fortress built by William the Conqueror. It is the
oldest royal residence still in use.

less German. He decided on the name Windsor, and the
Windsor dynasty has ruled Britain ever since.

As he aged, King George V grew more and more con-
cerned about his son, who would become king after him.
George V once remarked, "After I am dead, the boy will

ruin himself in twelve months." In fact, it took even less than a year.

George V died in 1936, and his son, upon becoming King Edward VIII, was bored with his official duties. He preferred to spend his time with a twice-divorced American woman named Wallis Simpson, whom he intended to marry.

King George V

Among government ministers and officials of the Church of England, a heated debate raged over whether or not marriage to a divorced woman was appropriate for a king of Britain. Since Henry VIII's reign in the 1500s, the British monarch has also served as head of the Church of England, a duty that made the question of Edward's behavior especially pronounced.

Finally, Prime Minister Stanley Baldwin bluntly told Edward that the people considered Wallis Simpson unfit to be queen. Ten days later, King Edward VIII announced his abdication (resignation from the throne), boarded the battleship H.M.S. *Fury,* and sailed into the misty English Channel. Edward later married Wallis Simpson, and the two spent the rest of their lives in exile as the Duke and Duchess of Windsor.

Edward VIII's younger brother immediately became King George VI. In Edward's abdication speech on December 11, 1936, he had pointed out that George "has one matchless blessing, enjoyed by so many of you and not bestowed on me—a happy home with his wife and children."

The dashing King Edward VIII and his American bride, Wallis Simpson, for whom he gave up the British throne

Princess Elizabeth waves from Buckingham Palace in 1937. She is surrounded by Princess Margaret, Queen Elizabeth, and newly crowned King George VI.

George VI's wife was the charming Elizabeth Bowes-Lyon, and their children were the princesses Elizabeth and Margaret Rose. Elizabeth had been born on April 21, 1926. She had no expectation of becoming queen until Edward VIII's abdication. When their father returned home the day he became king, Elizabeth and Margaret Rose curtseyed to him instead of throwing their arms around him and kissing him as usual. After she learned that her father was to be king, Elizabeth told her sister that she might one day be queen. Margaret Rose replied, "Poor you."

Elizabeth, who had been known to her family as "Lilibet" since childhood, grew up with the interests and activities of the countryside. She loved horses and became a good rider. She also loved dogs, especially little Welsh corgis.

Elizabeth's education was supervised by her mother, who hired a governess named Marion Crawford to watch over the two princesses. The girls called her Crawfie. Tutors visited the palace to teach Elizabeth history and the twists and turns of the unwritten constitution of Great Britain. She was also tutored in languages and music but proved skillful at neither.

Once Elizabeth became heir to the throne, her father took an active role as well. He helped her read *Punch,* a popular journal that satirized British politics; this introduced her to personalities and events in a lighthearted way. He also showed her articles from London's popular newspaper, the *Times.* With Crawfie, she studied the

Royal Collection of Art. Her studies were supplemented by museum trips with her grandmother, Queen Mary.

Elizabeth's mother "thought one could take formal education too seriously." Both parents were pleased that she was unsophisticated and not bookish. Lessons were often cut short, in fact, so that the princesses could play with their horses or dogs or just tramp around outside.

But World War II put an end to her cloistered life. Throughout the war, able-bodied citizens pitched in to help the war effort. Britons mobilized into fire brigades, rescue units, and home guard forces to watch for Germans along the coasts of the British Isles. Women volunteered to work in munitions factories or drive ambulances.

Elizabeth and Margaret enjoying some hacking on horseback on Elizabeth's fourteenth birthday

Margaret looks on as Elizabeth addresses
British children in a radio broadcast
during World War II.

At the start of the war in 1939, Elizabeth was just
thirteen years old, but she desperately wanted to take
part in the war effort. She knitted scarves for soldiers at
the front; she bought war bonds; and, at age fourteen,
she made her first radio broadcast to the children of
Britain. "We are all trying to do all we can to help our

gallant sailors, soldiers, and airmen," she said, "and we are trying, too, to bear our share of the danger and sadness of war. We know in the end all will be well."

Despite her efforts, Elizabeth, staying outside of London at Windsor Castle, felt far from the war. She had been sent to live there during the war, while the king and queen braved the bombs at Buckingham Palace, a royal residence in London. Things livened up for the girls, however, when German bombers targeted Windsor while the king and queen were visiting. No one was hurt in the attack, but the royal chapel was flattened.

Elizabeth claimed that she could now understand the sufferings of other Britons whose homes had been bombed. Tragedy also hit the royal family: On August 25, 1942, Elizabeth's uncle George, the Duke of Kent, was killed in a plane crash while touring bases of the Royal Air Force. The royal family, like other English families, was also subject to food and clothes rationing. But Elizabeth did not mind wearing old dresses or eating a little less. In fact, she became noted for her thrift.

When Elizabeth turned eighteen, King George finally gave in to her persistence and allowed her to join the ATS. Like all the other girls in the ATS, she learned to drive and repair jeeps and trucks. She was finally getting her hands dirty, changing oil and tires.

Rescue workers evacuate a victim of
Germany's bombing campaign against
London during World War II.

Elizabeth delighted in her new role and stuck with
it until the Germans surrendered on May 7, 1945 (called
V-E Day, for victory in Europe). During the victory celebrations, Elizabeth appeared on a balcony of Buckingham Palace with her parents and Prime Minister Winston
Churchill. She was dressed in her ATS uniform, waving
cheerfully at a country permanently changed by war.

Philip Mountbatten
wearing the insignia
of the Royal Navy

II

ELIZABETH REGINA

War had permanently changed Britain, and it had changed Elizabeth, too. Just before the war she had met the dashing young Prince Philip of Greece, who was serving in the British Royal Navy. She wrote to him during the war and he visited the royal family when on leave from the navy. By war's end, she found herself very much in love.

At first, King George refused to acknowledge that Lilibet had grown into a serious-minded princess of marriageable age. In March 1944, when the relationship became serious, George wrote, "We both think she is too young for that now as she has never met any young men of her own age." The king stalled as long as he could, but Philip was slowly being taken into the royal family.

Lord Louis Mountbatten, Philip's uncle and a trusted advisor to the king, worked tirelessly to secure Philip's marriage to Elizabeth. He helped arrange for Philip to adopt British citizenship. And later, when Philip renounced connections with Greece, he took his uncle's family name to replace his lost titles—Prince Philip of Greece became Lieutenant Philip Mountbatten of the British Royal Navy.

Philip proposed to Elizabeth in the summer of 1946 and she accepted, but the news was kept from the public at first. Elizabeth toured South Africa with her parents in early 1947, where, on her twenty-first birthday, she broadcast a message of optimism on BBC radio to British subjects everywhere. When they returned, King George gave his consent to the marriage, and the engagement was publicly announced.

Unfortunately, 1947 was not a good year for King George. After World War II, British colonies around the world moved toward independence. In 1947 alone,

King George granted independence to Pakistan, Burma (now called Myanmar), Ceylon (now called Sri Lanka), and India, which was known as the jewel in the crown of the British Empire because of the vast wealth of the Indian subcontinent. King George could not help seeing Elizabeth's marriage as another personal loss.

But Elizabeth's marriage provided a much-needed boost to British citizens. England was still in a bleak state of austerity caused by the financial strains of war. Food and clothing were still rationed in 1947, but Elizabeth was to be allotted extra rations for a wedding dress and a cake! On the eve of the wedding, the king granted Philip the title Duke

Elizabeth in her wedding dress

of Edinburgh and the right to be called "His Royal Highness." On November 20, 1947, Elizabeth and Philip were married in London's Westminster Abbey. Elizabeth sent her bridal bouquet to be placed on the Tomb of the Unknown Soldier.

After their wedding, Elizabeth and Philip began to make public appearances. The young, handsome couple was wildly popular. In December 1948, Elizabeth gave birth to her first son, Charles. These were happy days for the royal family.

Having lived through World War II, Elizabeth knew how important her obligations to the British public were. From an early age, she was introduced to the nitty-

Only a year after her marriage, Elizabeth gave birth to Charles, Prince of Wales and heir to the throne. In raising her family, the queen stressed the middle-class virtues of domesticity, thrift, and hard work.

gritty workings of the monarchy. The king received a pile of official communications from Parliament every day. Starting in the early morning the king reviewed the official mail in his "boxes," and more and more Elizabeth was allowed to look on.

But King George's deteriorating health cast a dark shadow over the next couple of years. In 1952, he was scheduled to make a five-month royal visit to Australia and New Zealand. Too sick to make the journey himself, he sent Elizabeth and Philip in his stead. The king saw them off at the airport and waved good-bye as the wind blew his hair into disorder. Elizabeth feared leaving her ailing father, but her duties as a representative of the British government came first.

The first stop for Elizabeth and Philip was the British colony of Kenya in East Africa. The couple stayed in a hunting lodge in the African countryside, where they observed the daily visits of animals to a nearby watering hole. Elizabeth filmed the animals with a home-movie camera. She was enjoying the trip when a telegram arrived with bad news—King George VI was dead. Heart trouble and lung cancer had killed Elizabeth's father on February 6, 1952.

Elizabeth and Philip canceled the trip to Australia and New Zealand and flew directly home for the king's funeral. Elizabeth had become queen as soon as her father died, but the crowning would not occur until the next year.

Elizabeth's sorrow was enormous, yet she had little time to grieve as her new responsibilities pressed in around her. She took the official oath, the Declaration of Accession, publicly proclaiming the start of her reign:

> My heart is too full for me to say more to you today than that I shall always work, as my father did throughout his reign, to uphold the constitutional Government and to advance the happiness and prosperity of my peoples, spread as they are the world over. I know that in my resolve to follow his shining example of service and devotion, I shall be inspired by the loyalty and affection of those whose Queen I have been called upon to be and by the counsel of their Parliaments.

The new queen found herself swept into a routine that would continue throughout her reign. She now received the "boxes" containing official documents, and she began to sign papers "Elizabeth R" (the R stands for *regina,* the Latin word for queen). To smooth the transition to the new reign, she kept her father's advisors and secretaries. "I want everything to continue exactly as it did with my father," she proclaimed.

The eccentric and electrifying Prime Minister Winston Churchhill, shown here at his desk in 1944, buoyed the queen's early reign by his tireless support.

She was briefed on parliamentary sessions every evening, and she met with Prime Minister Winston Churchill every Tuesday. Churchill had been turned out of office in 1945, but he returned to serve again from 1951 to 1955.

Elizabeth inherited a throne severely limited in real political power. She is little more than a uniting symbol in a constitutional monarchy. The queen cannot make laws; this is the responsibility of Parliament. Unlike a president or a prime minister, she cannot show favoritism to any one political party. Her political voice is only expressed, as historian Walter Bagehot put it, "to advise and warn." For example, the queen expresses her advice and opinions in her weekly meeting with the prime minister, but he is not obliged by law to act on her wishes. (So far in her reign, Elizabeth has presided over the governments of ten prime ministers, from Winston Churchill to Tony Blair.)

She could not have asked for a more kindly or sympathetic prime minister than Churchill to help her adjust to her new tasks. Churchill was an ardent monarchist and was as devoted to Elizabeth as he had been to her father. Elizabeth asked his advice on many questions. He advised her to take up residence in Buckingham Palace, though she was intimidated by its monstrous size and gloomy atmosphere. Although there are a number of royal residences in London, Buckingham Palace is the traditional home of monarchs. She and Philip employed decorators to make the palace more comfortable for themselves and their children.

Buckingham Palace,
the queen's home in London

The queen and most of her advisors were quite traditional, but she soon realized the need to keep the
monarchy in step with the general public. This would, in
fact, become one of the most important factors in the

evolving monarchy, despite Walter Bagehot's warning against letting in "daylight on magic."

When the British Broadcast Corporation (BBC) proposed to televise Elizabeth's coronation (crowning), she agreed, overruling her advisors and looking past her own shyness. Her grandfather, George V, had been the first monarch to broadcast on radio (in 1932), and Elizabeth decided that new technologies should, indeed, be used to let a little light in on the magic.

After months of preparation, the Archbishop of Canterbury, the highest-ranking religious official of the Church of England, lowered the St. Edward's Crown onto Elizabeth's head on June 2, 1953, in London's Westminster Abbey. Her full title as the sixty-second

Queen Elizabeth at her coronation with the orb and scepter, symbols of state

ruler of England was read aloud: "Elizabeth the Second, by the Grace of God of the United Kingdom of Great Britain and Northern Ireland and of Her other Realms and Territories Queen, Head of the Common Wealth, Defender of the Faith."

Later that same day, the BBC announced that Edmund Hillary, a New Zealand mountaineer, had become the first man to reach the summit of Mount Everest in the Himalayas, the highest mountain on earth. Hillary planted a British flag in the ice.

Great optimism met the start of the queen's reign. People were looking past the war toward a prosperous future. Because of Elizabeth's youth, comparisons were soon being made between her and her namesake, Elizabeth I, who ruled from 1558 to 1603, an era that saw the flourishing of English influence in both world politics and the arts.

Many also compared her to Queen Victoria, who ruled from 1837 to 1901, and they predicted another Victorian Age of stability and confidence. As Winston Churchill put it, "I whose youth was passed in the august, unchallenged and tranquil glare of the Victorian era, may well feel a thrill in invoking once more the prayer and anthem 'God Save the Queen.' "

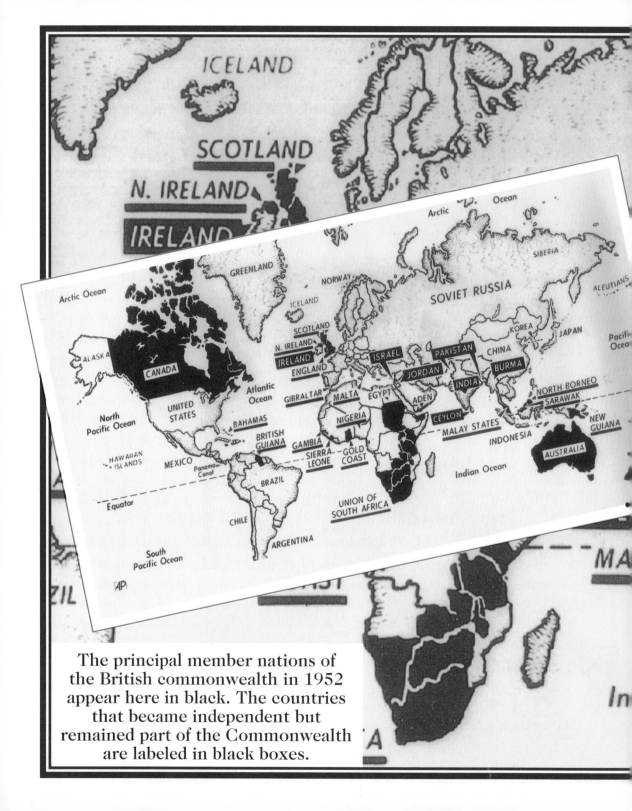

The principal member nations of the British commonwealth in 1952 appear here in black. The countries that became independent but remained part of the Commonwealth are labeled in black boxes.

III
The Queen and the Commonwealth

Elizabeth, as queen of Great Britain, is also head of the Commonwealth. While in South Africa shortly after her accession, during the winter of 1953–1954, she declared, "My whole life, whether it be long or short, shall be devoted to your service and the service of the great Imperial Commonwealth to which we all belong."

The Commonwealth is a unique association of countries (and territories dependent on them) that is held together by the common acceptance of the British monarch as its leader. The nature of the Commonwealth is constantly evolving. When the British could no longer hold back the sweeping nationalism that led to the independence of many colonies after World War II, they helped orchestrate a peaceful transition to self-government. Many former colonies joined the Commonwealth.

Some member states, such as Australia, Canada, and New Zealand, still pledge allegiance to Queen Elizabeth, although they are independent from British control. Most Commonwealth countries, however, are republics with their own heads of state. All member states acknowledge Elizabeth as head of the Commonwealth. Above all, the association is bound together by a common historical heritage and common interests, such as the belief in free trade.

Elizabeth has always kept herself well informed of the activities of the member states, and she has surprised prime ministers during their weekly meetings with her detailed knowledge of international events. The queen views her Commonwealth duties as a sacred trust that she inherited from her father. She retains real power in directing the course of the Commonwealth.

When Sir Anthony Eden (left) became
ill in 1957, Elizabeth named Harold Macmillan
(right) as his replacement, although the public
expected Eden's supporter R. A. Butler to be chosen
instead. The resulting stir baffled the queen, who
had acted according to tradition.

There are also certain reserve powers, known as
Royal Prerogatives, that Queen Elizabeth still wields.
She has sometimes stirred up controversies by exercising these powers. For example, in 1953, when Princess
Margaret informed the queen that she wished to marry
Peter Townsend, a distinguished World War II flying ace,

Elizabeth was shocked to discover that Townsend was a divorced man. Under the Royal Marriages Act of 1772, Elizabeth would have to give permission for Margaret to marry, unless Margaret was willing to give up her income and titles. The Church of England did not officially recognize the divorce, and the queen did not fully consent to the match, so Margaret had to give up Townsend.

The exercise of another Royal Prerogative, the queen's right to confirm the prime minister's election, was usually just a formality. When she exercised the right in 1957, though, it caused many to feel indignant. Conservative prime minister Anthony Eden had resigned suddenly due to failing health. R. A. Butler had been Eden's stand-in, and the public expected Butler to succeed Eden. But the queen learned that the Conservatives preferred Harold Macmillan over Butler, so she chose Macmillan. The queen had acted according to tradition, but it appeared to some that she was being manipulated by Parliament.

The Labour Party, the second major party in Parliament, had for some time elected their own party leader in order to avoid these complications. In 1965, the Conservative Party followed suit, eliminating the possibility that the queen would again be drawn into party politics. Since then, the queen has confirmed the leader of whichever party wins a general election.

Elizabeth
has struggled
to maintain the
image of regal
authority through
the turbulent world
changes that have
occurred during
her reign.

Many Britons felt that Queen Elizabeth had been old-fashioned in the handling of Princess Margaret's relationship with Peter Townsend and that her views did not reflect the changing morality of the nation. The controversy surrounding the appointment of the Conservative leader led more people to feel that the queen was out of touch. In spite of her efforts at modernization, she often seemed two steps behind the times.

As Queen, Elizabeth has had to balance matters of state with her family life. This family photo was taken shortly before her forty-second birthday and shows (from left) Philip and their children Anne, Edward, Charles, and Andrew, plus one of the queen's Welsh corgis.

IV
The Silver Jubilee

The popularity of a British monarch generally reflects the national mood. When times are good and Britain is triumphant in some endeavor or another, the monarch's popularity usually rises.

Although Great Britain was victorious in World War II, the economy was weakened by the war. British prestige in the world was declining. The United States, on the other hand, grew into a world industrial giant as a result of the war.

Soviet Marshall Joseph Stalin, U.S. President
Franklin Delano Roosevelt, and British Prime
Minister Winston Chruchill met in Tehran, Iran,
in 1943, to discuss Allied strategy for the defeat
of Hitler in World War II. The United States and
the Soviet Union emerged from the war as dominant
world powers, but Britain, racked by war debts,
suffered a sharp decline in world prestige.

The United States was being hailed as a superpower. The only other country that had earned that title was the Soviet Union, which was led by a Communist government. The competition between the United States and the Soviet Union for political dominance led to the long Cold War, in which virtually every other nation on earth allied itself with one side or the other. As a result of the rise of American power and the onset of the Cold War, British influence in international affairs fell off. This spurred anti-monarchists to attack the queen with great vigor.

As all the questions of Royal Prerogative and British influence were being tossed about, Elizabeth and Philip were also raising a family. They had three more children after Prince Charles: Princess Anne (born August 15, 1950), Prince Andrew (born February 19, 1960), and Prince Edward (born March 10, 1964). Elizabeth has been faced with the twin tasks of being monarch and mother. She once commented that bringing up children is hard "whether you are famous or quite unknown."

She had been protective of her children and attempted to keep the press out of their lives. She wanted them to have a normal childhood. Consequently, they were not allowed to be called "Your Highness" or other royal addresses; they were called simply by their names.

Her children were sent away to school. Philip insisted that Charles attend his old schools Cheam and Gordonstoun before entering the University of Cambridge in 1967. At Cambridge, Charles delighted the press on one occasion when he announced that he wanted to join the Labour Party. He was quickly informed that a constitutional crisis could erupt, and the prince shelved his political views.

People enjoyed Charles's encounters with the public, but the royal family was painfully aware of their sinking popularity. Philip, who referred to the royal family as "the firm," recognized the need for self-promotion and prodded Elizabeth to step up their public relations campaign as if they were running a private company. This was new ground for Elizabeth, who had always tried to keep the press at a distance.

The queen's response surprised everyone. She granted the BBC permission to make a two-hour documentary of royal life. The film, called *Royal Family,* aired in 1969, just before Prince Charles was officially crowned Prince of Wales, the traditional title for the male heir to the British throne. Both the film and Charles's crowning were good opportunities to put some sparkle back into the royal family's image.

But in Wales, those who desired independence from British rule had been gaining support and threatening

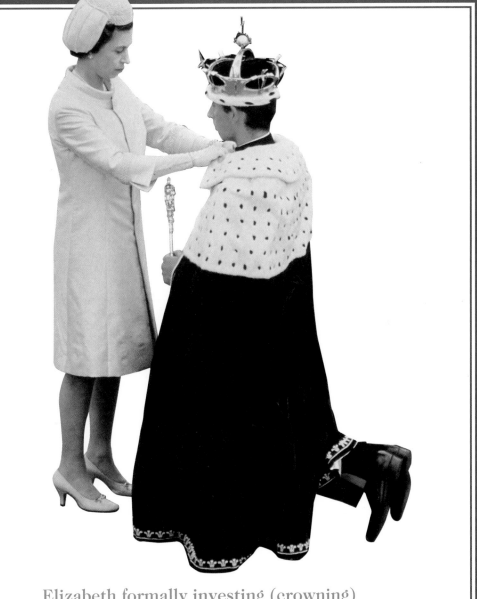

Elizabeth formally investing (crowning)
Charles with the title Prince of Wales,
making him heir to the throne, at
Caernarvon Castle in Wales on July 1, 1969

Elizabeth stops to talk with children in
St. Paul's Churchyard following her Silver Jubilee
thanksgiving service. These "walkabouts" are
the cause of great anxiety to the security
forces assigned to guard her.

violence. In the face of this danger, the queen presented
her beloved son to the Welsh at Caernarvon Castle on
July 1, 1969. Security was tight, and the ceremony
passed without incident.

Charles's crowning was widely televised, and the people loved it, but the queen's public appearances had changed. Her enemies were more willing to use violence and threats of violence against her, and the British press was more likely to print unfavorable news.

In 1971, the queen received a death threat as she prepared to open the annual parliamentary session. The houses of Parliament were searched for bombs. Nothing was found, but security measures were tightened. In some situations those responsible for the queen's safety have asked her to keep her distance from the public. Elizabeth has said, though, that her subjects have a right to see their queen in person.

Elizabeth was approaching her Silver Jubilee—her twenty-fifth year as queen—an occasion when she must be accessible to her subjects. In 1977, Elizabeth and Philip celebrated the Jubilee by walking through London's streets amid throngs of loyal supporters. Despite the troubles of the previous few years, the public's affection for her was still clear. Elizabeth smiled widely and told them, "It means so much to me."

In other parts of her realm, especially in Northern Ireland, some of her subjects were not so happy to be under British rule. For generations, British monarchs had passed the "Irish troubles" on to their successors.

Funerals for victims of political violence have
become commonplace in Northern Ireland.
A vicious sectarian conflict has raged there since
the partition of Ireland in 1922, which left the
six counties of Ulster under British rule.

Britain still rules the six counties of Northern Ireland
known as Ulster. The majority of the populace of Ulster
is Protestant and favors British rule, but many among
the Catholic minority would prefer to sever connections

with the British and join the Republic of Ireland. The conflict between the Republican (anti-British) and the Unionist (pro-British) factions has often turned violent.

A Republican terrorist organization known as the Irish Republican Army (IRA) threatened to assassinate Queen Elizabeth should she dare to visit Ulster as part of the Silver Jubilee celebrations. The Queen replied pluckily that she "was crowned Queen of the United Kingdom, Great Britain, and Northern Ireland." She proceeded with her tour, visiting the sights and people of Ulster amid bomb blasts and an occasional gunshot.

The British police force in Northern Ireland and the Queen's own secret service agents prevented the IRA from harming her. On August 27, 1979, however, the IRA struck close to her heart: IRA terrorists bombed a fishing boat off the Irish coast, killing Philip's uncle, Lord Mountbatten. Prince Charles had been especially fond of him. In a shaky voice, Charles said at Mountbatten's funeral service in Westminster Abbey, "I adored him. . . . I still cannot believe that I am standing here delivering an address about a man who, to me, always seemed reassuringly indestructible."

It was Prince Charles who gave the sagging image of the monarchy another shot in the arm by announcing his engagement to Lady Diana Spencer. Queen Elizabeth

Prince Charles and Princess Diana greet
the public after their wedding in 1981. Millions
of people around the world followed the
events of this storybook wedding.

had begun to worry about her son's marriage prospects
as he passed his thirtieth year still a single man. She was
worried because the future of the monarchy depended
on the direct continuation of the family line. But when
Charles and Diana were married at London's St. Paul's

Cathedral on July 29, 1981, the queen and the public were elated by what looked like a fairy-tale romance. The couple became international celebrities overnight.

Diana became the royal family's most valuable asset. She was outgoing and relaxed in a way that neither Elizabeth nor Charles were. It seemed suddenly that Diana was everywhere. Her face appeared on the covers of almost every news and fashion magazine.

What seemed like a fairy tale, though, was just a break in the declining popularity of the monarchy. The royal family was just entering its most disastrous days. Elizabeth's position as queen of Britain would be challenged in the coming years by a rapidly changing Britain and changes in her own family.

British Prime Minister Margaret Thatcher's
conservative economic policies drew attention
to the lavish spending of the royal family.
The public was having its own financial
hardships and cried out against the cost to
taxpayers of royal privileges.

V

An Uncertain Future

In 1979, the British elected their first woman prime minister, Margaret Thatcher. Thatcher was a conservative who believed that Britain's expensive health care and welfare systems should be pared down, and she moved toward privatizing some of these services. In the 1980s, Britain experienced a difficult transitional period:

unemployment rose sharply, and strikes among industry workers caused economic instability.

Thatcher's policies created problems for Queen Elizabeth. As Thatcher reduced government spending, people talked about how the queen received millions of pounds sterling (British currency) annually for nothing except being queen. It was also pointed out that the queen did not pay taxes.

To make matters worse for the queen, Thatcher, the daughter of a lower middle-class greengrocer, said that honors and awards should be given only to those who merited them. This was rather awkward for Elizabeth, who was queen only because she was the king's eldest child. Thatcher also believed that Queen Elizabeth should work as an ambassador for British business, especially to forge closer ties with the United States and the European Economic Community, on which Britain's finances depend.

The differences between the queen and Thatcher came out in July 1986 when the Commonwealth Games, a series of sporting events open to Commonwealth participants, were to be held in Britain. Thirty-one Commonwealth countries boycotted the games because of Thatcher's reluctance to levy sanctions on South Africa, a member of the Commonwealth.

Queen Elizabeth wears a kiwi feather Maori cape and
observes the work of students at a woodcarving
school during her visit to the Commonwealth country
of New Zealand in 1995. Throughout her reign,
she has been a tireless ambassador for international
trade and unity among Commonwealth countries.

South Africa was at that time ruled by a white minority government that barred the black majority from full
political participation. The queen was in favor of the

sanctions, partly because there are more nonwhite than white countries in the Commonwealth. Queen Elizabeth has always been sensitive to race questions; she once described the Commonwealth as an "equal partnership of nations and races."

Commonwealth countries, however, have expressed their own grievances against Queen Elizabeth. In New Zealand, the Maori people—the original inhabitants—had organized to protest the seizure of their lands by British settlers. Queen Elizabeth encountered some Maori protesters at one village in New Zealand, and one Maori dropped his pants and exposed his backside in her direction. In Australia, where anti-monarchist sentiment had also been growing, Queen Elizabeth was struck at point-blank range by an egg.

In February 1992, Queen Elizabeth received another stinging insult in Australia, not from a random protester this time but from Australian prime minister Paul Keating. Royal protocol demands that no one physically touch the queen; Keating actually put his arm around Elizabeth's waist, and while doing so he hinted that Australia would be a republic by the year 2000. The queen was outraged by his impertinence.

When Queen Elizabeth returned to Britain she received reports that Charles and Diana's marriage was

The marriage of Prince Charles and
Princess Diana crumbled amid lurid tabloid
journalism, but there is hope that the dignity
of the royal family will be restored with
Elizabeth's grandchildren Harry and William.

crumbling. She might have been reminded of Bagehot's
writings on the monarchy that she had read as a child:
"Above all things our royalty needs to be reverenced. . . . We
have come to regard the Crown as head of our *morality.*"

The fire at Windsor Castle in 1992 caused
extensive damage. When it was proposed that
the taxpayers foot the bill, many Britons argued
that the queen, who is one of the richest people in
the world, did not deserve public assistance.

Was the queen, after a lifetime of dutiful service to her
subjects, going to see the monarchy undermined by the
behavior of her own children?

Fate also seemed to turn against the queen: On the morning of November 20, 1992 (Elizabeth and Philip's forty-fifth wedding anniversary), a fire broke out at Windsor Castle. When the last embers were finally extinguished and inspectors appraised the damage, they estimated that it would cost 60 million pounds (about $90 million) to repair the castle.

The fire occurred during a tough economic time in Britain. Also, the American magazine *Forbes* had just ranked Queen Elizabeth as the sixth richest woman in the world. The nation entered a debate over who should pay for the damages, and whether the royal family or the whole nation owned the castle to begin with. One columnist in the *London Times* commented, "While the castle stands, it is theirs, but when it burns down, it is ours."

The burning of Windsor revealed that Britons were not willing to blindly follow the queen. Overwhelmingly, the public demanded that the royal family help cover the costs of the damages. Four days after the fire, Elizabeth addressed the nation with unusual candor: "1992 is not a year I shall look back on with undiluted pleasure. In the words of one of my more sympathetic correspondents, it has turned out to be an *annus horribilus* [Latin for "horrible year"]."

Queen Elizabeth volunteered to begin paying taxes shortly after this speech, but only on part of her income. And she agreed to open Buckingham Palace temporarily to the public, with the proceeds of tours going toward the repairs at Windsor.

These actions were intended to appease the queen's critics. But the dire state of Britain's economy prevented many from sympathizing with a privileged and wealthy woman. The entire episode represented a low point in British national self-esteem.

In December 1992, it was officially announced that Prince Charles and Princess Diana had separated, and by 1995 there was talk of divorce. Surely Elizabeth must have been reminded that an unacceptable marriage arrangement had forced Edward VIII to abdicate during her childhood. Princess Anne had also been divorced and remarried, and Prince Andrew's marriage to Sarah Ferguson was crumbling.

It has been reported that Charles has told his mother that he fears he will not be king. Perhaps the British will find Prince William, Charles and Diana's eldest son, to be an acceptable substitute. Or the nation may decide that Queen Elizabeth II, a dutiful and traditional monarch, should be the last reigning sovereign of Great Britain.

Queen Elizabeth in the
twilight of her reign waves to
her adoring American fans
on a visit to Texas.

In 1991, a bill was introduced into the Houses of Parliament proposing to abolish the monarchy and "establish a democratic, federal and secular Commonwealth of England, Scotland and Wales." The bill was strongly defeated, but talk of the abolition of the monarchy has become commonplace in Britain.

Britain has had a monarch for more than a thousand years. Queen Elizabeth II can trace her descent back to Edgar, king of England in the late tenth century. The queen also witnessed the survival of Britain's monarchy during World War II, a time when many other monarchies perished.

Queen Elizabeth has always defended her role and her British subjects. She is a matter-of-fact queen and a representative of middle-class traditions, such as family and duty to one's country. Her reign and the monarchy itself have been called into question, but so far she has weathered many tests. Even the most ambitious republicans, anxious to be governed entirely by elected representatives in Parliament, realize that Elizabeth's legacy may be uncertain, but Britain will not part with its present queen.

FOR MORE
INFORMATION

Hall, Trevor. *The Royal Family :at Home and Abroad.* With photographs by David Levenson. Codalming, Surrey, England: Colour Library Books, 1989.

Jay, Antony. *Elizabeth R: The Role of the Monarchy Today.* With photographs by David Secombe. London: BBC Books, 1992.

For Advanced Readers

Cannon, John, and Ralph Griffiths. *The Oxford Illustrated History of the British Monarchy.* New York: Oxford University Press, 1989.

Flamini, Roland. *Sovereign: Elizabeth II and the Windsor Dynasty.* New York: Delocorte Press, 1991.

Harris, Kenneth. *The Queen.* New York: St. Martin's Press, 1994.

On Video

Elizabeth R. London: BBC Video, 1992. Distributed by BBC Lionheart Television. Insights into the activities of the Queen and the Royal Family; includes official occasions plus personal and family events.

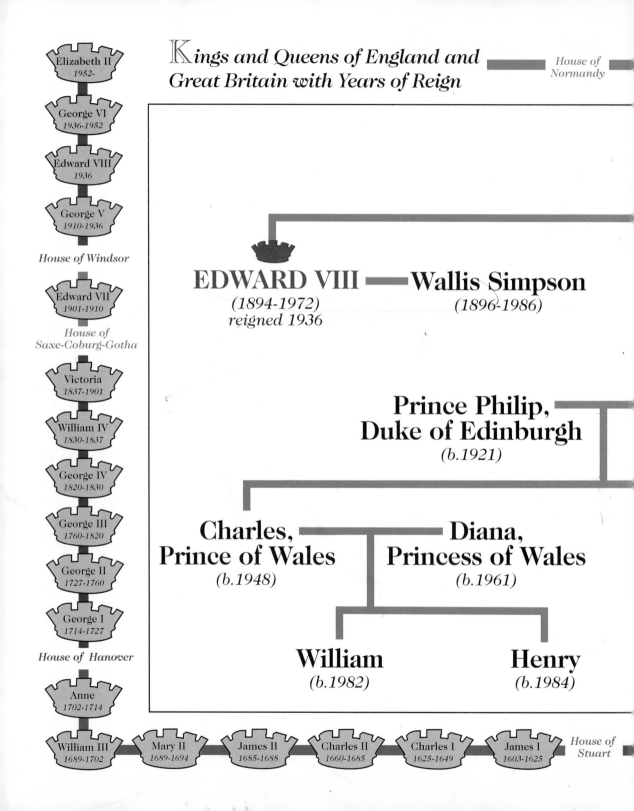

Kings and Queens of England and Great Britain with Years of Reign

House of Normandy

Elizabeth II
1952-

George VI
1936-1952

Edward VIII
1936

George V
1910-1936

House of Windsor

Edward VII
1901-1910

House of Saxe-Coburg-Gotha

Victoria
1837-1901

William IV
1830-1837

George IV
1820-1830

George III
1760-1820

George II
1727-1760

George I
1714-1727

House of Hanover

Anne
1702-1714

William III
1689-1702

Mary II
1689-1694

James II
1685-1688

Charles II
1660-1685

Charles I
1625-1649

James I
1603-1625

House of Stuart

EDWARD VIII
*(1894-1972)
reigned 1936* — **Wallis Simpson**
(1896-1986)

Prince Philip, Duke of Edinburgh
(b.1921)

Charles, Prince of Wales
(b.1948) — Diana, Princess of Wales
(b.1961)

William
(b.1982) ## Henry
(b.1984)

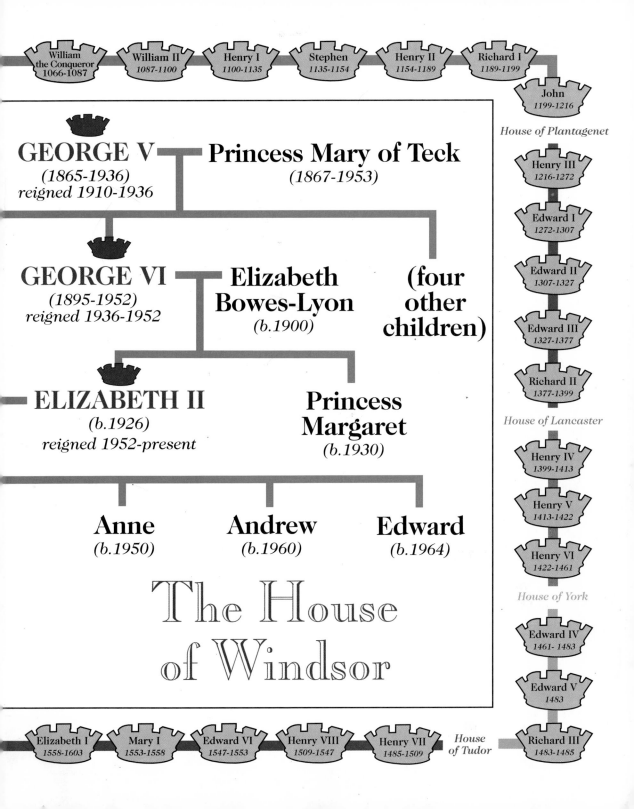

William the Conqueror
1066-1087

William II
1087-1100

Henry I
1100-1135

Stephen
1135-1154

Henry II
1154-1189

Richard I
1189-1199

John
1199-1216

House of Plantagenet

Henry III
1216-1272

Edward I
1272-1307

Edward II
1307-1327

Edward III
1327-1377

Richard II
1377-1399

House of Lancaster

Henry IV
1399-1413

Henry V
1413-1422

Henry VI
1422-1461

House of York

Edward IV
1461- 1483

Edward V
1483

Richard III
1483-1485

GEORGE V
(1865-1936)
reigned 1910-1936

Princess Mary of Teck
(1867-1953)

GEORGE VI
(1895-1952)
reigned 1936-1952

Elizabeth Bowes-Lyon
(b.1900)

(four other children)

ELIZABETH II
(b.1926)
reigned 1952-present

Princess Margaret
(b.1930)

Anne
(b.1950)

Andrew
(b.1960)

Edward
(b.1964)

The House of Windsor

Elizabeth I
1558-1603

Mary I
1553-1558

Edward VI
1547-1553

Henry VIII
1509-1547

Henry VII
1485-1509

House of Tudor

INDEX

Page numbers in *italics* refer to illustrations.

Andrew, Prince, *36,* 39, 56
Anne, Princess, *36,* 39, 56
Auxiliary Territorial Service
    (ATS), *7,* 16–17

Baldwin, Stanley, 10
Buckingham Palace, 26,
    26–27, 56
Butler, R. A., 33, 34

Caernarvon Castle, *41,* 42
Charles, Prince of Wales, 22,
    36, 39, 40, *41,* 45, *46,*
    46–47, 52, 54
Churchill, Winston, 17, *25,*
    26, 29, *38*
Commonwealth, *30,* 31–32,
    50
Coronation, *28,* 28
Crawford, Marion, 13

Declaration of Accession, 24
Diana (Spencer), Princess,
    45–47, *46,* 52, *54*

Eden, Sir Anthony, *33,* 34
Edgar, King of England, 58
Edward, Prince, *36,* 39
Edward VIII, 10–11, *11*
Elizabeth I, 29
Elizabeth II, Queen of England
    as ambassador, 20, 23,
      50–52
    birth of, 12
    coronation, 28–29
    education, 13
    images of, *12, 14, 15, 21,*
      35, 36
    marriage, 21–22
    in World War II, 7–8, 15–17

Ferguson, Sarah, 56

George, Duke of Kent, 16
George V, 8–10, *10*
George VI, 11, *12,* 23

Harry, Prince, *54*
Hillary, Edmund, 29

Irish Republican Army (IRA),
    45

Keating, Paul, 52

Macmillan, Harold, *33*, 34
Margaret, Princess, 12, *12,*
    14, 15, 33–35
Monarchy, 37–39, 58
Mountbatten, Louis, Lord, 20
Mountbatten, Philip. *See*
    Prince Philip.

New Zealand, *51*
Northern Ireland, *44*, 44–45

Parliament, 8, 26, 58
Philip, Prince, *18*, 19–22, *36*,
    40, 45
Political parties, 34

Roosevelt, Franklin Delano,
    38

Royal Marriages Act, 34
Royal Prerogatives, 33–34, 39

Silver Jubilee, *42*, 43
Simpson, Wallis, 10, *11*
St. Edward's Crown, 28
Stalin, Joseph, *38*

Thatcher, Margaret, *48,*
    49–50
Townsend, Peter, 33–35

Ulster (Northern Ireland),
    44–45
United States, 37–39

Victoria, Queen, 29

Westminster Abbey, 22, 29
William, Prince, *54*, 56
Windsor Castle, *9, 53*, 55
World War II, 7–8, 14–17,
    37, 38

About the Author

Robert Green is a freelance writer who lives in New York City. He is the author of *"Vive la France": The French Resistance during World War II* and biographies of important figures of the ancient world: *Alexander the Great, Cleopatra, Hannibal, Herod the Great, Julius Caesar,* and *Tutankhamun,* all for Franklin Watts. He has also written biographies of Queen Elizabeth I and King George III.